101 SHARK JOKES

by
Phil Hirsch

PYRAMID NEW YORK

TO
CAPTAIN STEVE
of the *Fantasea*,
his mate
LIL
and to
TRUDY
and
MEL...
who was once
almost thrown to the sharks!

101 SHARK JOKES
A PYRAMID BOOK

Pyramid edition published January, 1976
Sixth printing, August 1976

Library of Congress Catalog Card Number: 75-27240

Printed in the United States of America

Pyramid Books are published by Pyramid Publications (Harcourt Brace Jovanovich, Inc.). Its trademarks, consisting of the word "Pyramid" and the portrayal of a pyramid, are registered in the United States Patent Office.

PYRAMID PUBLICATIONS
(Harcourt Brace Jovanovich, Inc.)
757 Third Avenue, New York, N. Y. 10017

How do you recognize a shark owner in a pet shop?

He's the one buying a two-mile leash!

Whom do sharks hire to tidy up after them?

Mermaids!

Where is a shark's favorite spot to land on in Monopoly?

Free sharking!

How did the shark become so rich?

They discovered oil slicks on his property!

What did the shark do when he met the octopus?

He shook its hand, hand, hand, hand, hand, hand, hand, hand!

Why did the shark cross the road?

To get to the other tide!

Do sharks have good memories?

Yes, they never forget elephant jokes!

Why do sharks have large mouths?

So they can eat submarine sandwiches— containing real submarines!

Why are sharks stupid?

They refuse to stay in schools!

Which fish have lots of money?

Loan sharks!

Top Shark Movies

GONE WITH THE FINNED

IT HAPPENED ONE BITE

THE GRAD-YOU-ATE

THE CHEWS OF THE FISHERMAN

DEATH WASH

BUTCHERED CASSIDY AND
THE SUNDANCE KID

THE BEST FEARS OF OUR LIVES

DEATH OF A SAILSMAN

THE SHARKSKIN OF OUR TEETH

FIVE QUEASY PIECES

FINNY LADY

MAIM

THE AWFUL TOOTH

THE GOT-FATHER

Do sharks ever come up for air?

Only when they want to feel like a fish out of water!

What's the most effective shark-repellent known?

The Sahara Desert!

Who doesn't have to worry about the Better Business Bureau inspecting his merchandise?

A used-shark dealer!

What happened when Charlie the tuna fled from the shark?

He became chicken of the sea!

What happened to the pearl diver who ate alphabet soup?

A shark took the words right out of his mouth!

How can you tell if there's a shark in your bathtub?

You can't—take showers!

How are sharks served in restaurants?

At a table, like everyone else!

What makes an ideal shark breakfast?

Captain Crunch!

To a shark, what is the most embarrassing moment?

Being mistaken for a minnow by the Jolly Green Giant!

Why do sharks dislike Coca-Cola?

Because it's the reel thing!

What is the national homeland for sharks?

Fin-land!

What do married sharks do when they have a fight?

They sleep in separate waterbeds!

What do you call an underwater billiard player?

A pool shark!

When do sharks favor stricter zoning laws?

When their next-door neighbor's a crab!

Who is the shark's favorite bandleader?

Dock Severinson!

What sign makes a shark very happy?

No fishing!

What hobby does a shark like?

Anything it can sink its teeth into!

Why do sharks detest gangsters?

They always carry a rod!

Why do sharks tear into pirates?

Because they love plank-steak!

What did they say about the fisherman who waded into a sea full of sharks?

He was fishing in troubled waters!

Why was the fisherman disappointed even though he caught 20 porgies, 17 flounders, 15 bluefish, 13 snappers, 12 sharks, 8 mackerels, and 7 sea bass?

Because he was fishing for the halibut!

How does a shark see a doctor?

It stows away on a hospital ship!

Why are drowning sharks always left to die?

Who'd want to give them mouth-to-mouth resuscitation?

Why did the shark refuse to attack Mark Spitz when he tried to swim the Atlantic?

Because he was only a Spitz in the ocean!

When sharks need an operation, which doctor will they visit?

Any qualified sturgeon!

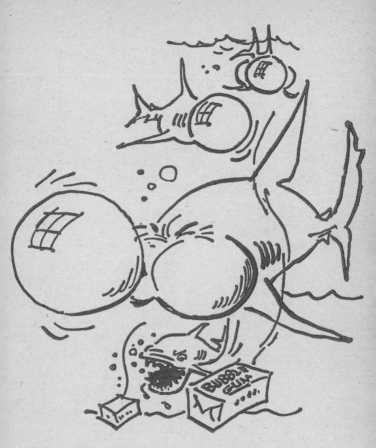

What happened when the sharks nibbled on the cargo ship carrying gum?

They bit off more than they could chew!

What old-time comic do sharks laugh at most?

Groucho Sharks! (But they hate his brother —Harpoon!)

What's soft, yellow, and very, very dangerous?

Shark-infested custard!

How do sharks play hockey?

Just like everybody else, except the winning team eats the losers!

How do you get six sharks in a Volkswagen?

Three in the front and three in the back!

Why are sharks considered bad-mannered?

They bite the hand that feeds them!

What's a good spread-on shark repellent?

Peanut butter—a shark doesn't like eating things that stick to its mouth!

Where do sharks live in Canada?

Sharkatchewan!

What did the school art teacher teach her class of sharks?

How to jaw!

What shark is in the Bible?

Noah's shark!

Why did the shark topple the light house?

He needed a new flashlight!

What does a shark order in a restaurant?

A chef salad!

What do you call a shark's signature?

A jaw-to-graph!

How big is the largest shark in the world?

A little biggger than the second largest one!

What do French sharks call ham?

Jawbon!

Why don't sharks like to play football?

They can't stand being on the line!

Do sharks speak French?

No, they know no "merci!"

What shark plays hockey for the Boston Bruins?

Brad shark!

How do you stop a school of sharks from charging?

Take away their credit cards!

What will a shark eat in a grocery store?

The grocer!

How do you make a shark float?

Two scoops of ice cream, a shark, and some root beer!

What did the critics think about the horror movie, JAWS?

It was a real sharker!

How do sharks get so relaxed?

From chewing what comes naturally!

How can you tell the difference between a shark and a tuna?

If you don't know, stay out of the ocean!

Do sharks like to act in movies?

Only if they get big, juicy parts!

How do sharks kiss?

Very carefully!

Why couldn't the shark stay home at night?

It was married to a crab!

What character in literature is most hated by sharks?

Captain Hook!

Why did the shark wear red suspenders?

The blue ones broke!

How does a referee start a swimming race in fishland?

"On your sharks . . . !"

How did the fish win the sharks' beauty contest?

Don't ask—it must have been a fluke!

Why do sharks detest tennis?

They refuse to get too close to the net!

What's the toughest job a shark has?

Finding a dentist who'll see him twice a year

Who said sharks really know how to hurt a guy?

The one-legged water skier!

What did the shark say to taunt the scuba diver holding a speargun?

"You couldn't hit the side of a barnacle!"

Which revolutionary war hero do the sharks admire most?

Nathan Hale-ibut!

With the sharks lurking nearby, what did the mermaid say to the boyfriend who had recently broken off their engagement?

"Come on in, the water's fin!"

Why was inventor Thomas Alvah Edishark famous?

He built a better mouth-trap!

What did the sharks do when Jackie Gleason fell into the water?

Chewed the fat!

Why did so many sharks refuse to see the movie "Jaws" when it first opened?

The admission price was $3.50, and even for a shark, that's too big a bite!

Now that he is a Hollywood celebrity, how is the star of the movie "Jaws" doing?

Swimmingly!

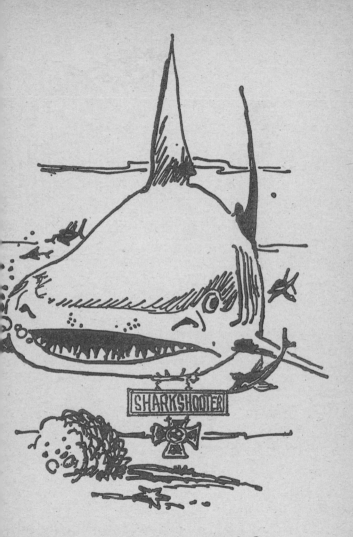

What rifle award can sharks win?

Sharkshooter!

What do you call a shark from Tennessee?

A Chattanooga chew-chew!

TV GORED

Top Tv Shark Shows
Time: SUNDAY, BLOODY SUNDAY

WHAT'S MY LINE

SCAR TREK

THE PRICE IS BITE

SCREAM TENNIS

GRAB-IT AND COSTELLO

MARY TYLER NO-MOORE

FATHER GNAWS BEST

THE DAME OF THE WEEK

I SCREAM OF JEANNIE

MONTY PYTHON'S DYING CIRCUS

YOU BAIT YOUR LIFE

ROMPER RUIN

JOHNNY SCARSON

GAM*BIT*

MOTHERS-IN-JAW

I SHOVE LUCY

HUCKLEBERRY HOUNDED

ONE LIFE TO LIVE

MERV GRIF-FINNED

TOOTH OR CONSEQUENCES

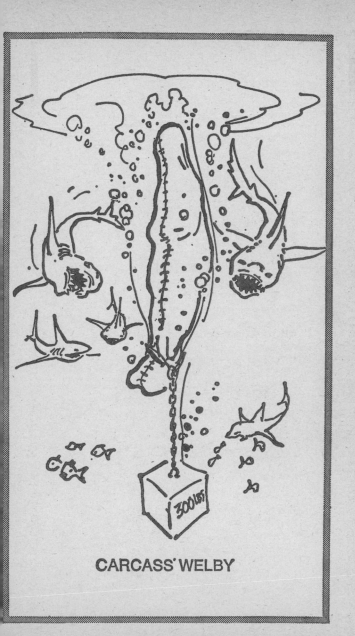

CARCASS' WELBY

BARNABY BONES

MASTERPIECES THEATER

RHODA-ROOTERED

ROCKY THE DYING SQUIRREL

EDGE OF FRIGHT

THE GAL-GULPING GOURMET

LET'S MAKE A SQUEAL

JEOPARDY!

POLICE GORY

M*A*S*H*E*D

HAWAII FIVE, OH!

CELEBRITY TROLLING

GLADYS KNIGHT AND THE SHIPS

THE WAY IT WHIRS

THE SMOTHERED BROTHERS

Do you know the sharks' favorite ice cream flavors?

Toothy-fruity and sharkolat!

Why did the sharks refuse to attack the Glasgow crew when they took over the ship in a mutiny against their captain?

Because the one flavor they dislike is bitter-Scotch!

IQ Test: The Three Musketeers, weaponless, found themselves stranded in mid-ocean and attacked by man-eating sharks. What swam by to enable them to fight off the sharks?

Swordfish, of course!

What do you call a shark hunter who uses a pea shooter?

Stupid!

What does a shark panhandler do?

He puts the bite on people!

When do old shark fighters quit?

When they run out of old sharks to fight!

To whom will a shark never tell a secret?

A big-mouthed bass!

What does Cinderella Shark wear?

Glass flippers!

Why did the shark bite off the mast of a sailboat?

It needed a toothpick!

Why was the shark standing on its head?

It was watching "The Poseidon Adventure"!

What do sharks eat with peanut butter?

Jellyfish!

What sharks make good carpenters?

Hammerheads!

What do sharks have that no other fish have?

Baby sharks!

What day of the week do sharks hate most?

Fryday!

What do they call the man who stuck his hand into the shark's mouth?

Lefty!

How do you keep sharks from smelling?

You cut off their noses!

Why did the shark swallow Elton John?

Because it went for him hook, line and singer!

What did the librarian use for sharkbait?

A bookworm!

by Fred Wolfe

SHARK SURVIVAL GUIDE

1. Use the "buddy" system. **If a shark ap-proaches—throw him your buddy.**

2. Bore him to death. Force him to listen to a speech by any politician.

3. **Distract** him. Show him **the centerfold of**
"Anglers' Magazine."

4. If he's a great *Red* shark—tell him you hate John Wayne and love Billy Jack.

5. Hold up a large mirror. Then the shark will think *he's* being attacked!

6. Fail to use your "Five-Day Deodorant" pad for at least 15 days—then flap your armpits at the shark!

7. Put on **a** Kissinger mask and arbitrate
   with the shark.

8. Look the shark straight in the eye—with binoculars—from a mountaintop!

9. For the optimist, carry a protest sign and picket.

10. Move to the Sahara Desert!

11. Strap a fin on your back and pretend you're just another shark.

12. Show the shark a notarized statement that you're "chicken"—and swearing that Colonel Sanders rates you as finger-lickin' bad!

What's big and gray and has a trunk?

A shark going on a trip!

Why did the shark cross the road?

To get to the other tide!

What did the shark do after his Saturday night bath?

He left a ring around the ocean!

What has the most fiendish fish of all contributed to the auto industry?

Shark absorbers!

What happened when the shark swallowed the ship's fuel tanks?

It got gas pains!

What did the mother shark tell her child when it began to chase the man in circles?

Don't play with your food!

Where did the shark see *"The Exorcist"*?

In the Devil's Triangle!

Who is the most famous author in shark-land?

William Sharkespeare!

Why did the shark spank the naughty channel marker?

Because it was a bad buoy!

How did the sailor survive after his boat sank in shark-infested water?

He used a bar of soap to wash himself ashore.

What did Liberace the Shark do when his baby grand didn't sound right?

He called the piano tuna!

If you're in the path of a hungry shark, what should you feed it?

Jaw breakers!